Waiting on God

Geary Reid

ISBN: 978-976-8305-71-8

Acknowledgments

Great thanks must be expressed to the following people:

The heavenly Father, for granting me the wisdom and inspiration to record the information in this book, which I began on November 23, 2021, and completed on November 26, 2021; my family, for their continued encouragement and support regarding various challenges; and several people who have assisted with reviewing and editing the book:

- Pastor Jocelyn Dolphin
- Rendell F. Harry

To you, the reader: have fun while reading, and grasp and practice what you learn so that this world will become a better place. Many people are depending on your guidance. We all need a shoulder to lean on and a hand to guide us.

Rev. Geary Reid
MBA, FCCA, FAAPM, MPM, CAT

Reid's Learning Institute and Business Consultancy

reidnlearn.com

Amazon: amazon.com/author/gearyreid

Facebook: Reid n Learn

Instagram: Reid n Learn

LinkedIn: Reid's Learning Institute and Business Consultancy

199 Kuru - Kururu, Soesdyke Linden Highway
Guyana, South America

Table of Contents

Introduction

God will bless those who wait on him. While the time of waiting may look long, it is always outweighed by the blessings of God. Waiting on God must never be considered a waste of time, but an opportunity for God to do what he is better at doing.

Too many persons are struggling while trying to do the works of the Lord. However, if they stand back, they will see the power and salvation of God. Believers must not be anxious for anything, as God has everything covered and will bless those who wait on him. Waiting on God does not mean that persons must be idle, as God always wants persons to be occupied in his work as they wait for him to come through for them.

When God promised to bless Abraham, it appeared to Abraham and Sarah that God was taking too long. However, God came through for them, and Sarah's temporary barrenness was over as God blessed them with Isaac. Through Isaac, God was able to fulfill his words to Abraham.

Waiting on God requires patience. Waiting on God requires faith. When believers exercise their faith in God, he will make impossible things happen for them.

As believers wait, they must pray and praise God. They may not have everything they need, but as they praise God, they are celebrating him for things that he has the ability to do. The prayers of believers will cause the sick to be healed, as they have faith in God to heal those they pray for.

Trusting God may seem difficult. However, persons must trust God, since only he knows the future. As persons trust him to work on their behalf, they must expect that great things will happen for them. They must learn not to give up.

Knowing the Word of God is a good foundation for all believers. Those who need his wisdom and knowledge must spend time in his presence as they wait on him. The knowledge of God is superior to man's knowledge, and God wants to bless persons with knowledge if they will seek him.

Those who wait on God can expect that he will increase their strength. They will soon mount up with wings like eagles. The Lord will prosper those who wait on him, and their days of poverty will be over as his blessings fill their lives.

The Lord knows the way and the timing to help his children, so they need to wait on him. The death of Lazarus troubled his family, but Jesus delayed his visit to Lazarus because he wanted to perform a miracle. Most likely, God is having you wait because he wants to do something great in and through your life. Therefore, wait upon the Lord.

1. Does God require persons to wait on him?

Some persons think that it takes too long to wait on God, so they believe that they must run ahead of him. Since persons cannot see God physically, they are often unsure if he is working on their behalf or if he has forgotten them.

When a person is able to interact with someone else face to face, they can spend time reasoning their concerns and observing the other person's non-verbal communication. When children ask their parents for something, they will look at their parents' facial expression and body language to assess if their request will be actioned. With God, however, persons cannot assess any physical actions from him, since he is a spirit.

1.1 God protects his children against their enemies

Believers are constantly reminded to trust God and wait for him to do what he has promised to do. Even when their friends, family, and enemies rise up against them, they need to wait on God. No believer is strong enough by themselves to withstand their enemies, but when they wait on God and allow him to defend them, then he will subdue their enemies.

Psalm 27:10-14

10 When my father and my mother forsake me, then the LORD will take me up. 11 Teach me thy way, O LORD, and lead me in a plain path, because of mine enemies. 12 Deliver me not over unto the will of mine enemies: for false witnesses are risen up against me, and such as breathe out cruelty. 13 I had fainted, unless I had believed to see the goodness of the LORD in the land of the living. 14 Wait on the LORD: be of good courage, and he shall strengthen thine heart: wait, I say, on the LORD.

The psalmist was quick to recognize that even parents will sometimes forsake their children, but the Lord will be there for those who trust him. Enemies are always there waiting to destroy believers, but when they wait on

God and ask him to lead them in the plain path, they can rest assured that God will take them through difficult situations without them being hurt, and he will make them victorious (Psalm 27:11-13).

As the psalmist thinks of what enemies can do to create harm, it can cause any believer to faint (Psalm 27:13). The problems can be great, but when God is on the side of the believers, he will always prove that he is bigger than all man's problems, and he will deliver his children.

1.2 No one has seen God, but he will defend his children

Isaiah 64:1-5

1 Oh that thou wouldest rend the heavens, that thou wouldest come down, that the mountains might flow down at thy presence, 2 As when the melting fire burneth, the fire causeth the waters to boil, to make thy name known to thine adversaries that the nations may tremble at thy presence! 3 When thou didst terrible things which we looked not for, thou camest down, the mountains flowed down at thy presence. 4 For since the beginning of the world men have not heard, nor perceived by the ear, neither hath the eye seen, O God, beside thee, what he hath prepared for him that waiteth for him. 5 Thou meetest him that rejoiceth and worketh righteousness, those that remember thee in thy ways: behold, thou art wroth; for we have sinned: in those is continuance, and we shall be saved.

In Isaiah 64:4, the conversation is very interesting, as it points to the fact that no one has heard or seen God from the beginning, yet those who have waited for God have seen him come through for them. God will not let his children down. So, if you are anxious and believe that he will not come through for you, just wait on God and he will do marvelous things in his time. Remember that God knows the ending from the beginning.

Isaiah 46:10-13

10 Declaring the end from the beginning, and from ancient times the things that are not yet done, saying, My counsel shall stand, and I will do all my pleasure: 11 Calling a ravenous bird from the east, the man that executeth my counsel from a far country: yea, I have spoken it, I will also bring it to pass; I have purposed it, I will also do it. 12 Hearken unto me, ye stouthearted, that are far from righteousness: 13 I bring near my righteousness; it shall not be far off, and my salvation shall not tarry: and I will place salvation in Zion for Israel my glory.

All humans are limited in their thinking and their abilities, but God sees the future. He knows what will happen to every human, and sometimes his attempts to get people to wait on him are because he wants to protect them from danger.

2. God fulfilled his promise with Abraham

God wants everyone to wait for him. This may sound too far-fetched. However, no one knows the future but God, so sinners and saints must wait on him. God's timing may look too long for man, but everyone must remain committed to God and wait. This world can be free from many problems if persons exercise patience and allow God to do what he knows is best.

2.1 Sarai did not want to wait anymore, so she gave Hagar to Abram

God had promised Abram and Sarai that they would have a child. It had been many years, and this promise had not come through. Both adults were probably frustrated, and they tried to see if they could help God. While they waited a long time, they thought of an alternative approach. Sarai, the wife of Abram, offered Hagar, her Egyptian slave, to sleep with Abram. This encounter resulted in Hagar becoming pregnant and giving birth to Ishmael, Abram's first child.

Genesis 16:1-16

¹Now Sarai Abram's wife bare him no children: and she had a handmaid, an Egyptian, whose name was Hagar. ²And Sarai said unto Abram, Behold now, the LORD hath restrained me from bearing: I pray thee, go in unto my maid; it may be that I may obtain children by her. And Abram hearkened to the voice of Sarai. ³And Sarai Abram's wife took Hagar her maid the Egyptian, after Abram had dwelt ten years in the land of Canaan, and gave her to her husband Abram to be his wife. ⁴And he went in unto Hagar, and she conceived: and when she saw that she had conceived, her mistress was despised in her eyes. ⁵And Sarai said unto Abram, My wrong be upon thee: I have given my maid into thy bosom; and when she saw that she had conceived, I was despised in her eyes: the LORD judge between me and thee. ⁶But Abram said unto Sarai, Behold, and thy maid is in thine hand; do to her as it pleaseth thee. And when

Sarai dealt hardly with her, she fled from her face. ⁷And the angel of the LORD found her by a fountain of water in the wilderness, by the fountain in the way to Shur. ⁸And he said, Hagar, Sarai's maid, whence camest thou? and whither wilt thou go? And she said, I flee from the face of my mistress Sarai. ⁹And the angel of the LORD said unto her, Return to thy mistress, and submit thyself under her hands.

¹⁰And the angel of the LORD said unto her, I will multiply thy seed exceedingly, that it shall not be numbered for multitude. ¹¹And the angel of the LORD said unto her, Behold, thou art with child and shalt bear a son, and shalt call his name Ishmael; because the LORD hath heard thy affliction. ¹²And he will be a wild man; his hand will be against every man, and every man's hand against him; and he shall dwell in the presence of all his brethren. ¹³And she called the name of the LORD that spake unto her, Thou God seest me: for she said, Have I also here looked after him that seeth me? ¹⁴Wherefore the well was called Beerlahairoi; behold, it is between Kadesh and Bered. ¹⁵And Hagar bare Abram a son: and Abram called his son's name, which Hagar bare, Ishmael. ¹⁶And Abram was fourscore and six years old, when Hagar bare Ishmael to Abram.

2.2 Sarah became angry with Hagar

It is often seen that when people choose not to wait on God and to make their own decision instead, they become angry (Genesis 16:6-9). It was Sarah who gave Hagar to Abraham for him to sleep with her (Genesis 16:2-3). However, after this, God fulfilled his promise in Genesis 21:1-6. The same woman whom Sarah offered to her husband had now become her own enemy, and Sarah did not want Hagar to be around her (Genesis 21:9-10). However, God was there to comfort Hagar and also to give a name to her son (Genesis 16:7-12). The Lord is always just to everyone. He demonstrated this to Hagar, since she did choose to go and sleep with Abraham, but her mistress had asked her to do so (Genesis 16:7-9). Jealousy started to rage, and Ishmael was mocking Isaac (Genesis 21:9). Whenever persons do not wait on God but try to go ahead of him, their own decisions often backfire on them (Genesis 21:9-21).

Genesis 21:7-21

⁷And she said, who would have said unto Abraham, that Sarah should have given children suck? for I have born him a son in his old age. ⁸And the child grew, and was weaned: and Abraham made a great feast the same day that Isaac was weaned. ⁹And Sarah saw the son of Hagar the Egyptian, which she had born unto Abraham, mocking. ¹⁰Wherefore she said unto Abraham, Cast out this bondwoman and her son: for the son of this bondwoman shall not be heir with my son, even with Isaac. ¹¹And the thing was very grievous in Abraham's sight because of his son. ¹²And God said unto Abraham, Let it not be grievous in thy sight because of the lad, and because of thy bondwoman; in all that Sarah hath said unto thee, hearken unto her voice; for in Isaac shall thy seed be called. ¹³And also of the son of the bondwoman will I make a nation, because he is thy seed.

¹⁴And Abraham rose up early in the morning, and took bread, and a bottle of water, and gave it unto Hagar, putting it on her shoulder, and the child, and sent her away: and she departed, and wandered in the wilderness of Beersheba. ¹⁵And the water was spent in the bottle, and she cast the child under one of the shrubs. ¹⁶And she went, and sat her down over against him a good way off, as it were a bow shot: for she said, let me not see the death of the child. And she sat over against him, and lift up her voice, and wept. ¹⁷And God heard the voice of the lad; and the angel of God called to Hagar out of heaven, and said unto her, what aileth thee, Hagar? Fear not; for God hath heard the voice of the lad where he is. ¹⁸Arise, lift up the lad, and hold him in thine hand; for I will make him a great nation. ¹⁹And God opened her eyes, and she saw a well of water; and she went, and filled the bottle with water, and gave the lad drink. ²⁰And God was with the lad; and he grew, and dwelt in the wilderness, and became an archer. ²¹And he dwelt in the wilderness of Paran: and his mother took him a wife out of the land of Egypt.

The Lord did not ill-treat Hagar nor Ishmael, but he demonstrated love over them (Genesis 21:14-21). Even when persons do not fulfill the will of God, he often extends mercy, not for them to live in sin, but for them to draw closer to him. With the two children of Abraham, Ishmael brought discomfort to Abraham, while Isaac brought comfort to him. When a person waits upon God, they will have joy, and they may even laugh in their old age to see what the Lord has done (Genesis 21:8).

The son that Abraham received with his wife Sarah was given a name by God, and his name was Isaac (Genesis 22:3). The Lord distinguished between Abraham's two sons: Ishmael would be called a nation, and Isaac would be his seed (Genesis 21:13)

2.3 Sarah became pregnant

The story of Abraham and Sarah giving birth to Isaac is well known. Sarah was barren for a long period of time. During her barrenness, Abraham bore a son with Hagar. However, Ishmael was not God's plan for Abraham, so God still had to fulfill his plan through Abraham and his wife. So, Sarah became pregnant and gave birth to Isaac. While Sarah and Abraham did not wait for God to fulfill his plan, the Lord still came through for them at a later stage. Waiting on God may be long, but he always fulfills his promises (Genesis 22:2).

Genesis 21:1-6

¹And the LORD visited Sarah as he had said, and the LORD did unto Sarah as he had spoken. ²For Sarah conceived, and bare Abraham a son in his old age, at the set time of which God had spoken to him. ³And Abraham called the name of his son that was born unto him, whom Sarah bare to him, Isaac. ⁴And Abraham circumcised his son Isaac being eight days old, as God had commanded him. ⁵And Abraham was an hundred years old, when his son Isaac was born unto him. ⁶And Sarah said, God hath made me to laugh, so that all that hear will laugh with me.

It took fourteen more years for God to fulfill his promise to Abraham to give him Isaac (Genesis 16:16, 21:5). God's timing is never the same as man's timing, so everyone must wait on him.

Figure 1. Ishmael was a son from Abraham and Sarah's decision, while Isaac was God's blessing to them

2.4 God worked with Isaac as Abraham's sacrifice

While Ishmael was older than Isaac, God used Isaac as the child that he wanted Abraham to offer as a sacrifice. When God has a plan for an individual, he will carry out his plan, because God believes in fulfilling his promises. It might have been a painful experience for Abraham to obey God and offer his only son as the sacrifice that God wanted. Nevertheless, Abraham was willing to obey God, so he took Isaac his only son to be sacrificed.

What a painful experience for any parent who had to wait so long to have a child. However, when persons honor God's request, their lives and the lives of their family will be blessed (Genesis 22:1-19).

Genesis 22:1-19

¹ And it came to pass after these things, that God did tempt Abraham, and said unto him, Abraham: and he said, Behold, here I am. ² And he said, Take now thy son, thine only son Isaac, whom thou lovest, and get thee into the land of Moriah; and offer him there for a burnt offering upon one of the mountains which I will tell thee of. ³ And Abraham rose up early in the morning, and saddled his ass, and took two of his young men with him, and Isaac his son, and clave the wood for the burnt offering, and rose up, and went unto the place of which God had told him. ⁴ Then on the third day Abraham lifted up his eyes, and saw the place afar off. ⁵ And Abraham said unto his young men, Abide ye here with the ass; and I and the lad will go yonder and worship, and come again to you. ⁶ And Abraham took the wood of the burnt offering, and laid it upon Isaac his son; and he took the fire in his hand, and a knife; and they went both of them together. ⁷ And Isaac spake unto Abraham his father, and said, my father: and he said, here am I, my son. And he said, behold the fire and the wood: but where is the lamb for a burnt offering? ⁸ And Abraham said, my son, God will provide himself a lamb for a burnt offering: so they went both of them together. ⁹ And they came to the place which God had told him of; and Abraham built an altar there, and laid the wood in order, and bound Isaac his son, and laid him on the altar upon the wood. ¹⁰ And Abraham stretched forth his hand, and took the knife to slay his son.

¹¹ And the angel of the LORD called unto him out of heaven, and said, Abraham, Abraham: and he said, here am I. ¹² And he said, lay not thine hand upon the lad, neither do thou anything unto him: for now I know that thou fearest God, seeing thou hast not withheld thy son, thine only son from me. ¹³ And Abraham lifted up his eyes, and looked, and behold behind him a ram caught in a thicket by his horns: and Abraham went and took the ram, and offered him up for a burnt offering in the stead of his son. 14 And Abraham called the name of that place Jehovah Jireh: as it is said to this day, in the mount of the LORD it shall be seen.

15 And the angel of the LORD called unto Abraham out of heaven the second time, 16 And said, by myself have I sworn, saith the LORD, for because thou hast done this thing, and hast not withheld thy son, thine only son: 17 That in blessing I will bless thee, and in multiplying I will multiply thy seed as the stars of the heaven, and as the sand which is upon the sea shore; and thy seed shall possess the gate of his enemies; 18 And in thy seed shall all the nations of the earth be blessed; because thou hast obeyed my voice. 19 So Abraham returned unto his young men, and they rose up and went together to Beersheba; and Abraham dwelt at Beersheba.

Over and over, when people wait on God, they will be doing something great for themselves. Remember that God will make his promise come to pass. God blessed the descendants of Abraham through his son Isaac, and many nations received such blessings.

Hebrews 11:17-19

17 By faith Abraham, when he was tried, offered up Isaac: and he that had received the promises offered up his only begotten son, 18 Of whom it was said, that in Isaac shall thy seed be called: 19 Accounting that God was able to raise him up, even from the dead; from whence also he received him in a figure.

2.5 Abraham is dead, but his name still lives on

Abraham is dead and gone, but his name lives on. God was willing to work beyond the sin that Abraham committed, and he blessed Abraham and his offspring.

Hebrews 6:13-15

13 For when God made his promise to Abraham, because he could swear by no greater, he sware by himself, 14 Saying, Surely blessing I will bless thee, and multiplying I will multiply thee. 15 And so, after he had patiently endured, he obtained the promise.

3. Waiting requires patience

Everyone who waits on God must exercise patience. God is not a microwave, where persons put whatever they need in it and then press the timer, and whatever is in the microwave is quickly heated. Oftentimes, it is seen that God works differently through his children.

God asked his children not to be anxious for anything. This does not mean that people must not have expectations of him. However, God wants people to be patient as he works on delivering whatever he knows is best for them. As persons exercise their patience, they must be prayerful and give thanks unto God.

Philippians 4:6-7

⁶Be careful for nothing; but in everything by prayer and supplication with thanksgiving let your requests be made known unto God. ⁷And the peace of God, which passeth all understanding, shall keep your hearts and minds through Christ Jesus.

Many times, when persons are anxious, they make wrong decisions. In their haste, they may not even consider the errors that they are about to make.

Consider this example, in which an individual needs a concrete house to be built. The construction of the building will start from the foundation. The contractor will place mortar into the dug-out earth surface, which will be used as the foundation of the building. Although the contractor will place some materials in the concrete mixture to make it harden faster, at least some time must be given for the mortar to draw strength. After the mortar draws strength and is ready to take the weight, then the contractor will add more building materials on that foundation. If the contractor were to place other building materials on the recent mortar after it was poured into the earth's surface, then the mortar would be destroyed and the foundation of the building would be compromised.

Just as people need to give some time for the materials that used in the foundation to be ready, they must also give God time to do his work. There are times when God will operate swiftly, but he will not be bullied by anyone, since he knows what he is doing.

Lamentations 3:26

26 It is good that a man should both hope and quietly wait for the salvation of the LORD.

God requires everyone to exercise patience in him, as he wants to do something great in their lives. He wants to add more blessings to their lives, but he wants them to be in a position to receive his blessings. Many believers want to run away from the period where the mortar has to become strong enough for material to be placed on it. After they run away from God's plan, they eventually find themselves doing more harm to themselves in the long run, as they did not give themselves enough time for their foundation to cure.

Patience allows believers to wait in God for the invisible things. When a person exercises patience, no one can measure their patience.

Romans 8:22-25

22 For we know that the whole creation groaneth and travaileth in pain together until now. 23 And not only they, but ourselves also, which have the first fruits of the Spirit, even we ourselves groan within ourselves, waiting for the adoption, to wit, the redemption of our body. 24 For we are saved by hope: but hope that is seen is not hope: for what a man seeth, why doth he yet hope for? 25 But if we hope for that we see not, then do we with patience wait for it.

When many persons are younger, they are excited for everything to be completed quickly. However, when those same persons become aged, they often begin to embrace patience. Sometimes, too much haste brings danger. However, those who exercise patience will see the benefits of waiting, since many great things may unfold due to the passage of time.

Farmers know that if they plant permanent trees, then they have to wait many years. While they wait for those permanent crops to produce their products, those farmers may plant some cash crops. The cash crops will produce quick results and may even allow the farmers to make money from those products that are sold. But when the permanent crops begin to bear, then they will bear for several years without the farmer having to do much to nurture them. God wants every believer to exercise patience like a farmer who has planted permanent crops and expects them to start producing several years after they were planted.

If a believer is patient with God, then they will receive blessing after blessing. Even in the nighttime season, God will bless them, because they are connected with him.

Psalm 30:5

5 For his anger endureth but a moment; in his favor is life: weeping may endure for a night, but joy cometh in the morning.

4. Waiting requires faith

Waiting on God is not a waste of time. Waiting on God does not require persons to be idle, but to exercise faith. When persons exercise faith, they are waiting on God to make those things which are not seen become visible to them. As believers exercise faith, they often challenge God to do something great for them.

When a person gives their heart to the Lord, they must be willing to exercise faith, since many of the things that they are expecting from God are invisible to the natural eye. They must remember that the world was formed by the command of God.

Hebrews 11:3

3 Through faith we understand that the worlds were framed by the word of God, so that things which are seen were not made of things which do appear.

Persons are saved through faith. Therefore, no one has any authority to boast about what they have done to obtain their salvation.

Ephesians 2:8-10

8 For by grace are ye saved through faith; and that not of yourselves: it is the gift of God: 9 Not of works, lest any man should boast. 10 For we are his workmanship, created in Christ Jesus unto good works, which God hath before ordained that we should walk in them.

4.1 Do persons need faith to serve God?

If anyone is going to serve God, then they must be prepared to walk in faith. There are many things they will not see in the natural, but through their spiritual eyes, and they must believe that God will make those things possible for them.

Hebrews 11:6

⁶ But without faith it is impossible to please him: for him that cometh to God must believe that he is, and that he is a rewarder of them that diligently seek him.

Figure 2. Without faith, persons will waste time, but with faith, God will reward them (Hebrews 11:6)

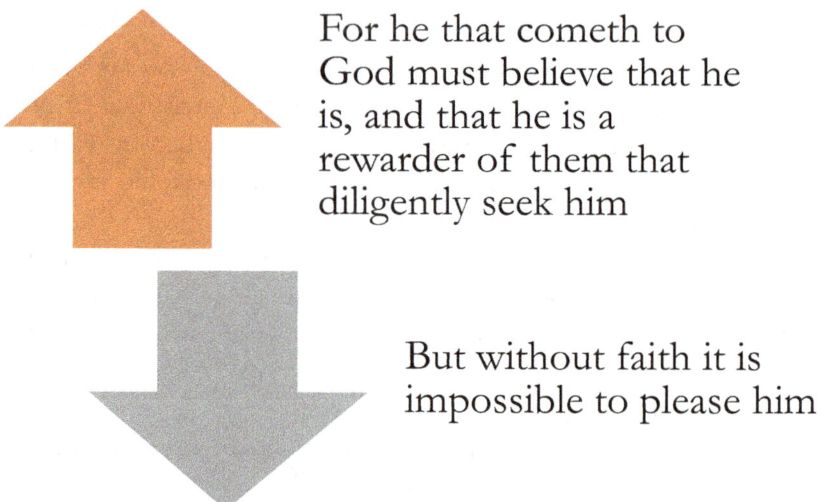

Without faith, persons are only wasting time when they are waiting. This time can be thought of as non-productive time. However, when persons wait on God through faith, they are placing their trust in God for him to work on their behalf. Hebrews 11:6 tells us that those who come to God must believe that he is a rewarder to them that diligently seek him. Therefore, persons who are exercising their faith must show diligence in God and not in themselves.

Figure 3. Faith requires confidence in God

It is God's desire to bless everyone. However, he wants persons to believe that he is their rewarder. Everyone, regardless of their knowledge and skills, must give God the reins to be in control over their lives.

4.2 Faith requires more than natural sight

While some things may appear impossible to the natural eyes, they will become possible as persons believe in the God who makes the impossible, possible. If persons see the things that they need, then why do they have to pray or trust God for those things? Hebrews 11:1 provides clarity about what faith is.

Hebrews 11:1

[1] *Now faith is the substance of things hoped for, the evidence of things not seen.*

Figure 4. Faith is the substance of things hoped for but not seen with the natural eyes

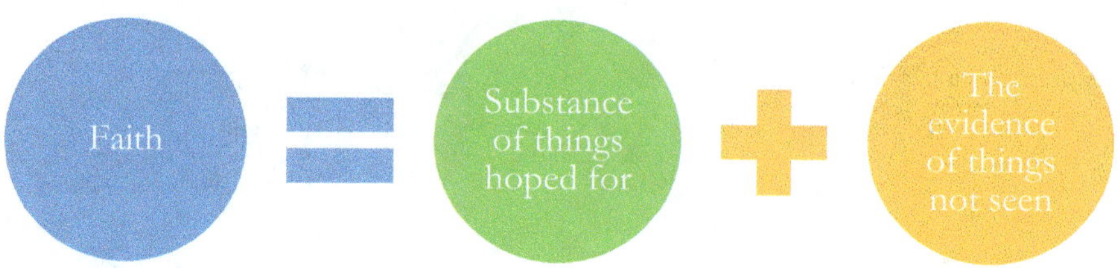

5. Waiting requires prayer

Waiting for God is something that every believer must do. As they wait for God, they must pray. Prayer has the ability to open many doors that are closed. Prayer heals the sick, according to James 5:15.

5.1 Nothing happens until believers pray

When believers sit down and do nothing, then nothing happens. However, when believers are active and prayerful, then great things will happen.

Matthew 7:7-8

7 Ask, and it shall be given you; seek, and ye shall find; knock, and it shall be opened unto you: 8 For every one that asketh receiveth; and he that seeketh findeth; and to him that knocketh it shall be opened.

5.2 Prayer of faith

God wants all believers to pray in faith. They must believe that whatever they pray for, as long as it is in accordance with God's word, it will be possible. When believers pray for sick persons, they must have faith that God will heal those persons and cause them to recover.

James 5:13-16

13 Is any among you afflicted? let him pray. Is any merry? let him sing psalms. 14 Is any sick among you? let him call for the elders of the church; and let them pray over him, anointing him with oil in the name of the Lord: 15 And the prayer of faith shall save the sick, and the Lord shall raise him up; and if he have committed sins, they shall be forgiven him. 16 Confess your faults one to another, and pray one for another, that ye may be healed. The effectual fervent prayer of a righteous man availeth much.

Whenever a person prays, but does not believe that God will cause their prayer to come through, then they will not have what they prayed for. So, persons must believe in God, pray, and wait for God to grant the desires of their hert.

5.3 Prayer moves mountains

Believers sometimes fail to recognize and utilize the power that they have. There are many obstacles standing in the way of believers, but all the believers have to do is pray to their powerful God. Jesus taught the disciples that if they have faith and pray, then even mountains will respond to their prayer (Matthew 21:21).

Matthew 21:18-21

18 Now in the morning as he returned into the city, he hungered. 19 And when he saw a fig tree in the way, he came to it, and found nothing thereon, but leaves only, and said unto it, Let no fruit grow on thee henceforward forever. And presently the fig tree withered away. 20 And when the disciples saw it, they marveled, saying, how soon the fig tree is withered away! 21 Jesus answered and said unto them, Verily I say unto you, If ye have faith, and doubt not, ye shall not only do this which is done to the fig tree, but also if ye shall say unto this mountain, Be thou removed, and be thou cast into the sea; it shall be done.

So, as believers wait on God, they must remain prayerful. They must keep praying until something good happens for them.

5.4 Prayer and praise makes things happen in the natural

When believers pray, they sometimes only think that things will happen in the spiritual realm. However, God will show up and make many things happen in the natural as they pray.

For example, Paul and Silas were in a physical prison. It was a difficult place to be in, especially as they had been doing the works of the Lord. As they were wrongfully incarcerated, they chose to pray and sing praises. When they did that, God heard them and did wonders for them. The things that God did to save Paul and Silas caused the prison officer to respect them and their God. The prison officer also asked what he must do to be saved by the same God who came to the rescue of Paul and Silas.

Acts 16:23-33

23 And when they had laid many stripes upon them, they cast them into prison, charging the jailor to keep them safely: 24 who, having received such a charge, thrust them into the inner prison, and made their feet fast in the stocks. 25 And at midnight Paul and Silas prayed, and sang praises unto God: and the prisoners heard them. ²⁶And suddenly there was a great earthquake so that the foundations of the prison were shaken: and immediately all the doors were opened, and every one's bands were loosed. ²⁷And the keeper of the prison awaking out of his sleep, and seeing the prison doors open, he drew out his sword, and would have killed himself, supposing that the prisoners had been fled. ²⁸But Paul cried with a loud voice, saying, Do thyself no harm: for we are all here. ²⁹Then he called for a light, and sprang in, and came trembling, and fell down before Paul and Silas, ³⁰and brought them out, and said, Sirs, what must I do to be saved? ³¹And they said, Believe on the Lord Jesus Christ, and thou shalt be saved, and thy house. ³²And they spake unto him the word of the Lord, and to all that were in his house. ³³And he took them the same hour of the night, and washed their stripes; and was baptized, he and all his, straightway.

If anyone thinks that prayer is ordinary, then they need to read Acts 16:23-33. God will go to extremes to save his children, and he showed that as he saved Paul and Silas from the prison. As believers pray, they must understand the power of agreement that is necessary for their prayers to be answered.

Figure 5. God's impact when Paul and Silas agreed in prison

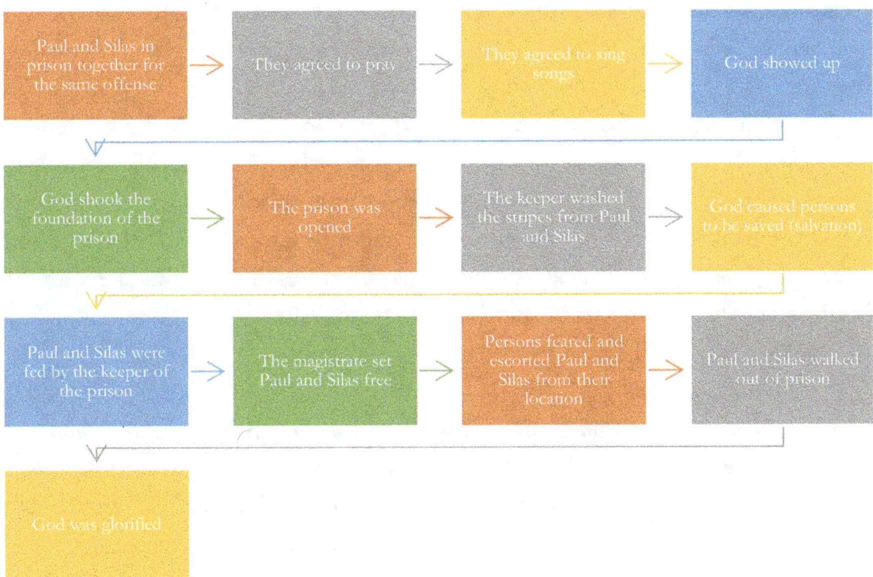

If believers have differences, they must learn to forgive each other. Once they forgive, then they can agree with each other and pray, and God will hear their prayer. Disagreements often hinder believers' prayers. Even though

Paul and Silas prayed and sang songs, if they were in disagreement, then God would have not heard their prayer. So, while believers wait, and pray, they must put aside their differences and agree, and then they will see God coming through for them, as he did for Paul and Silas.

Matthew 18:18-19

18 Verily I say unto you, Whatsoever ye shall bind on earth shall be bound in heaven: and whatsoever ye shall loose on earth shall be loosed in heaven. 19 Again I say unto you, That if two of you shall agree on earth as touching anything that they shall ask, it shall be done for them of my Father which is in heaven.

Agreement among believers will get God to work with them. If they have disagreement, then even if they spend many days and hours praying, they will waste their time, because there is division among them.

5.5 God heard and answered Jehoshaphat's prayer

Another classic example of prayer unto God that proved impactful is the prayer done by Jehoshaphat and the people of Judah. When Jehoshaphat prayed, God caused many things to happen in the natural to save his children. Word was received that the enemies were coming up against the children of Judah (2 Chronicles 20:2). When Jehoshaphat received this bad news, he was worried, as most humans would be (2 Chronicles 20:3-4). However, he knew his God, and he sought God's intervention.

Jehoshaphat went to the temple of God, and he prayed. As he prayed, he reminded the Lord about his goodness over the children of Judah and Jerusalem (2 Chronicles 20:5-9), but he did not withhold his concerns about the enemies that were coming to destroy them (2 Chronicles 20:10-12). The prayer of Jehoshaphat was so effective that God heard him while he was still in the temple praying, and God gave the children of Judah a word (2 Chronicles 20:13-17).

2 Chronicles 20:1-16

1 It came to pass after this also, that the children of Moab, and the children of Ammon, and with them other beside the Ammonites, came against Jehoshaphat to battle. 2 Then there came some that told Jehoshaphat, saying, There cometh a great multitude against thee from beyond the sea on this side Syria; and, behold, they be in Hazazontamar, which is Engedi. 3 And Jehoshaphat feared, and set himself to seek the LORD, and proclaimed a fast throughout all Judah. 4 And Judah gathered themselves together, to ask help of the LORD: even out of all the cities of Judah they came to seek the LORD.

⁵ And Jehoshaphat stood in the congregation of Judah and Jerusalem, in the house of the LORD, before the new court, ⁶ And said, O LORD God of our fathers, art not thou God in heaven? and rulest not thou over all the kingdoms of the heathen? and in thine hand is there not power and might, so that none can withstand thee? ⁷ Art not thou our God, who didst drive out the inhabitants of this land before thy people Israel, and gavest it to the seed of Abraham thy friend forever? ⁸ And they dwelt therein, and have built thee a sanctuary therein for thy name, saying, ⁹ If, when evil cometh upon us, as the sword, judgment, or pestilence, or famine, we stand before this house, and in thy presence, (for thy name is in this house,) and cry unto thee in our affliction, then thou wilt hear and help.

¹⁰ And now, behold, the children of Ammon and Moab and mount Seir, whom thou wouldest not let Israel invade when they came out of the land of Egypt, but they turned from them, and destroyed them not; ¹¹ Behold, I say, how they reward us, to come to cast us out of thy possession, which thou hast given us to inherit. ¹² O our God, wilt thou not judge them? for we have no might against this great company that cometh against us; neither know we what to do: but our eyes are upon thee.

¹³ And all Judah stood before the LORD, with their little ones, their wives, and their children. ¹⁴ Then upon Jahaziel the son of Zechariah, the son of Benaiah, the son of Jeiel, the son of Mattaniah, a Levite of the sons of Asaph, came the Spirit of the LORD in the midst of the congregation; ¹⁵ And he said, Hearken ye, all Judah, and ye inhabitants of Jerusalem, and thou king Jehoshaphat, Thus saith the LORD unto you, Be not afraid nor dismayed by reason of this great multitude; for the battle is not yours, but God's. ¹⁶ Tomorrow go ye down against them: behold, they come up by the cliff of Ziz; and ye shall find them at the end of the brook, before the wilderness of Jeruel.

5.6 God took over the war

God took on the war against the enemies of Judah (2 Chronicles 20:17). It must not be a surprise to the children of God that when they pray, God will defend them.

Figure 6. God's response to the prayer of the children of Judah (2 Chronicles 20:17)

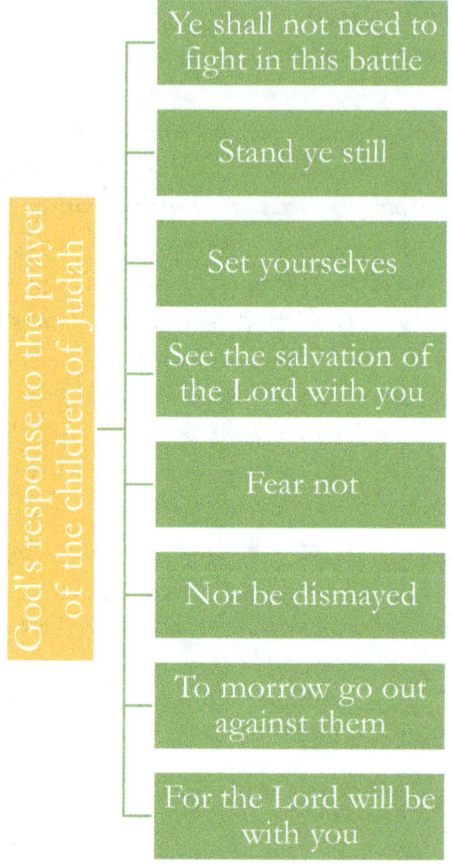

Anyone who prays to God and gets such a quick and detailed response must be relieved. The word of the Lord to the children of Judah was for them to take up their position, pray, and wait on him, and he would take over the battle and destroy the enemies. The children of Judah did not have to use any military weapon, since God was going to fight this war using different strategies.

2 Chronicles 20:17-30

17 Ye shall not need to fight in this battle: set yourselves, stand ye still, and see the salvation of the LORD with you, O Judah and Jerusalem: fear not, nor be dismayed; tomorrow go out against them: for the LORD will be with you.

¹⁸And Jehoshaphat bowed his head with his face to the ground: and all Judah and the inhabitants of Jerusalem fell before the LORD, worshipping the LORD. ¹⁹And the Levites, of the children of the Kohathites, and of the children of the Korhites, stood up to praise the LORD God of Israel with a loud voice on high. ²⁰And they rose early in the morning, and went forth into the wilderness of Tekoa: and as they went forth, Jehoshaphat stood and said, Hear me, O Judah, and ye inhabitants of Jerusalem; Believe in the LORD your God, so shall ye be established; believe his prophets, so shall ye prosper. ²¹And when he had consulted with the people, he appointed singers unto the LORD, and that should praise the beauty of holiness, as they went out before the army, and to say, Praise the LORD; for his mercy endureth forever. ²²And when they began to sing and to praise, the LORD set ambushments against the children of Ammon, Moab, and mount Seir, which were come against Judah; and they were smitten. ²³For the children of Ammon and Moab stood up against the inhabitants of mount Seir, utterly to slay and destroy them: and when they had made an end of the inhabitants of Seir, every one helped to destroy another. ²⁴And when Judah came toward the watch tower in the wilderness, they looked unto the multitude, and, behold, they were dead bodies fallen to the earth, and none escaped. ²⁵And when Jehoshaphat and his people came to take away the spoil of them, they found among them in abundance both riches with the dead bodies, and precious jewels, which they stripped off for themselves, more than they could carry away: and they were three days in gathering of the spoil, it was so much. ²⁶And on the fourth day they assembled themselves in the valley of Berachah; for there they blessed the LORD: therefore the name of the same place was called, the valley of Berachah, unto this day. ²⁷Then they returned, every man of Judah and Jerusalem, and Jehoshaphat in the forefront of them, to go again to Jerusalem with joy; for the LORD had made them to rejoice over their enemies. ²⁸And they came to Jerusalem with psalteries and harps and trumpets unto the house of the LORD. ²⁹And the fear of God was on all the kingdoms of those countries, when they had heard that the LORD fought against the enemies of Israel. ³⁰So the realm of Jehoshaphat was quiet: for his God gave him rest round about.

As God promised the children of Judah, he came through for them, and many nations feared them. God is still looking to come through for some believers who will pray and wait on him to give them victory. With God, nothing is impossible for him to do for his children.

6. Praise while waiting

Waiting on God is not a time for mourning, but a time to praise him. Even when believers do not yet have the victory at this stage, they must praise God. When believers go before the Lord to make their request, they must be in high spirits and praise their God.

Psalm 100:1-5

[1] Make a joyful noise unto the LORD, all ye lands. [2] Serve the LORD with gladness: come before his presence with singing. [3] Know ye that the LORD he is God: it is he that hath made us, and not we ourselves; we are his people, and the sheep of his pasture. [4] Enter into his gates with thanksgiving, and into his courts with praise: be thankful unto him, and bless his name. [5] For the LORD is good; his mercy is everlasting; and his truth endureth to all generations.

6.1 Praise God even when the enemies surround you

The enemies will surround the believers, but they must praise their God and not be afraid. They must leave their battles for God to fight for them, but in the meantime, they must give God praise.

Psalm 27:3-6

[3] Though an host should encamp against me, my heart shall not fear: though war should rise against me, in this will I be confident. [4] One thing have I desired of the LORD, that will I seek after; that I may dwell in the house of the LORD all the days of my life, to behold the beauty of the LORD, and to enquire in his temple. [5] For in the time of trouble he shall hide me in his pavilion: in the secret of his tabernacle shall he hide me; he shall set me up upon a rock. [6] And now shall mine head be lifted up above mine enemies round about me: therefore will I offer in his tabernacle sacrifices of joy; I will sing, yea, I will sing praises unto the LORD.

6.2 God is the believers' hiding place

As believers retreat and wait on God, they must continue to praise him. He is the hiding place for all believers and will preserve them during the time of difficulties.

Psalm 52:9

⁹ I will praise thee for ever, because thou hast done it: and I will wait on thy name; for it is good before thy saints.

Psalm 32:7-8

⁷ Thou art my hiding place; thou shalt preserve me from trouble; thou shalt compass me about with songs of deliverance. Selah. ⁸ I will instruct thee and teach thee in the way which thou shalt go: I will guide thee with mine eye.

6.3 God will subdue the believers' enemies

Those enemies of the believers may be many. However, God will subdue all enemies, as he has the power and might to take on an army and win.

Psalm 47:1-3

¹ O clap your hands, all ye people; shout unto God with the voice of triumph. ² For the LORD most high is terrible; he is a great King over all the earth. ³ He shall subdue the people under us, and the nations under our feet.

Psalm 46:1

¹ God is our refuge and strength, a very present help in trouble.

6.4 God is the believers' deliverer

The Lord will protect his children and deliver them, even in the time of trouble. There will be many afflictions against the believers, but God will step in for their defense (Psalm 34:15-21). Believers must praise the Lord at all times, and not only when things are going their way (Psalm 34:1-4). God has assigned angels to encamp round about his children. These angels will be there for the believers, even when the believers do not see the dangers that are hovering over their heads (Psalm 34:7).

Psalm 34:1-22

¹ I will bless the LORD at all times: his praise shall continually be in my mouth. ² My soul shall make her boast in the LORD: the humble shall hear thereof, and be glad. ³ O magnify the LORD with me, and let us exalt his name together. ⁴ I sought the LORD, and he heard me, and delivered me from all my fears. ⁵ They looked unto him, and were lightened: and their faces were not ashamed. ⁶ This poor man cried, and the LORD *heard him, and saved him out of all his troubles.* ⁷*The angel of the* LORD *encampeth round about them that fear him, and delivereth them.*

⁸*O taste and see that the* LORD *is good: blessed is the man that trusteth in him.* ⁹*O fear the* LORD, *ye his saints: for there is no want to them that fear him.* ¹⁰*The young lions do lack, and suffer hunger: but they that seek the* LORD *shall not want any good thing.* ¹¹*Come, ye children, hearken unto me: I will teach you the fear of the* LORD. ¹²*What man is he that desireth life, and loveth many days, that he may see good?* ¹³*Keep thy tongue from evil, and thy lips from speaking guile.* ¹⁴*Depart from evil, and do good; seek peace, and pursue it.*

¹⁵*The eyes of the* LORD *are upon the righteous, and his ears are open unto their cry.* ¹⁶*The face of the* LORD *is against them that do evil, to cut off the remembrance of them from the earth.* ¹⁷*The righteous cry, and the* LORD *heareth, and delivereth them out of all their troubles.* ¹⁸*The* LORD *is nigh unto them that are of a broken heart; and saveth such as be of a contrite spirit.* ¹⁹*Many are the afflictions of the righteous: but the* LORD *delivereth him out of them all.* ²⁰*He keepeth all his bones: not one of them is broken.* ²¹*Evil shall slay the wicked: and they that hate the righteous shall be desolate.* ²²*The* LORD *redeemeth the soul of his servants: and none of them that trust in him shall be desolate.*

There are even more reasons to praise the Lord as the believers hide in him and wait for him (Psalm 34:22). He has promised to protect them from destruction (Psalm 34:20). If believers understand how much God is protecting them and fighting for them, they will immediately start to praise him as they wait on him.

7. Trust God as you wait

Trusting God must not only be for financial benefit, but for every aspect of believers' lives. When persons are facing attacks from their enemies, they must also trust God. The arms of God are safe to protect those who trust him and wait on him to deliver them from the hands of their adversaries.

Psalm 56:1-13

1 Be merciful unto me, O God: for man would swallow me up; he fighting daily oppresseth me. 2 Mine enemies would daily swallow me up: for they be many that fight against me, O thou most High. 3 What time I am afraid, I will trust in thee. 4 In God I will praise his word, in God I have put my trust; I will not fear what flesh can do unto me.

5 Every day they wrest my words: all their thoughts are against me for evil. 6 They gather themselves together, they hide themselves, they mark my steps, when they wait for my soul. 7 Shall they escape by iniquity? in thine anger cast down the people, O God. 8 Thou tellest my wanderings: put thou my tears into thy bottle: are they not in thy book?

9 When I cry unto thee, then shall mine enemies turn back: this I know; for God is for me. 10 In God will I praise his word: in the LORD will I praise his word. 11 In God have I put my trust: I will not be afraid what man can do unto me. 12 Thy vows are upon me, O God: I will render praises unto thee. 13 For thou hast delivered my soul from death: wilt not thou deliver my feet from falling, that I may walk before God in the light of the living?

When believers call on their God, he will cause their enemies to turn back (Psalm 56:9). God has a way of confusing the enemies as he protects those who trust him. Many times, believers are not required to use physical weapons to fight their enemies, as they can allow their God to fight their battles (Psalm 56:10-13). Even when death seems certain for the believers, God will be there for those who trust him (Psalm 56:13).

7.1 God is the hiding place for believers

If believers leave themselves exposed to the attacks of their enemies, they will die. However, they can run to the Lord and be protected.

Proverbs 18:10

10 The name of the LORD is a strong tower: the righteous runneth into it, and is safe.

7.2 God's thoughts are superior to man's thoughts

The knowledge of God is superior to man's thinking. Therefore, every individual must rely on the wisdom of God, as he knows the way and will be there for them as they wait on him.

Isaiah 55:6-9

6 Seek ye the LORD while he may be found, call ye upon him while he is near: 7 Let the wicked forsake his way, and the unrighteous man his thoughts: and let him return unto the LORD, and he will have mercy upon him; and to our God, for he will abundantly pardon. 8 For my thoughts are not your thoughts, neither are your ways my ways, saith the LORD. 9 For as the heavens are higher than the earth, so are my ways higher than your ways, and my thoughts than your thoughts.

Romans 11:33

33 O the depth of the riches both of the wisdom and knowledge of God! how unsearchable are his judgments, and his ways past finding out!

People are often worried about the future. They blame God for taking too long, but they do not have a clue of what God is doing to protect and bless them. Do they have the same knowledge as God?

Ecclesiastes 8:17

17 Then I beheld all the work of God, that a man cannot find out the work that is done under the sun: because though a man labour to seek it out, yet he shall not find it; yea farther; though a wise man think to know it, yet shall he not be able to find it.

If even a man as wise as Solomon could not determine the works of the Lord, then everyone must leave God to do whatever he is doing as they wait on him.

Ecclesiastes 3:11

11 He hath made everything beautiful in his time: also he hath set the world in their heart, so that no man can find out the work that God maketh from the beginning to the end.

7.3 Those who trust God will receive his goodness

There is goodness in store for all those who trust the Lord. The Lord will hide those who trust in him from people who want to attack them.

Psalm 31:19-20

19 Oh how great is thy goodness, which thou hast laid up for them that fear thee; which thou hast wrought for them that trust in thee before the sons of men! 20 Thou shalt hide them in the secret of thy presence from the pride of man: thou shalt keep them secretly in a pavilion from the strife of tongues.

7.4 Trust him even when he offers correction

Every believer must trust God even when he corrects them or slays them. It is because of the love of God that he corrects his children and carries them through difficult situations.

Job 13:15

15 Though he slay me, yet will I trust in him: but I will maintain mine own ways before him.

7.5 Trust God and not the resources of men

Place trust in God and not in the resources of men. Men who go to war often place much trust in the ability of their weapons and their horses and chariots, but they must instead place their trust in God.

Psalm 20:7

7 Some trust in chariots, and some in horses: but we will remember the name of the LORD our God.

Men and other resources will fail, but God never fails. Therefore, trust him now and forever.

8. Be watchful as you wait

As believers wait on God, they must be watchful. They must have the expectation that God will come through for them. If they do not believe that God will work out things for them, then they are wasting time by waiting on him. It is God's intention to do good for those who believe and wait on him. He does not go back on his word, but will work to bring his promises to pass.

Numbers 23:19

19 God is not a man, that he should lie; neither the son of man, that he should repent: hath he said, and shall he not do it? or hath he spoken, and shall he not make it good?

8.1 God hears those who call on him

The Lord will hear those who call on him.

Micah 7:7

7 Therefore I will look unto the LORD; I will wait for the God of my salvation: my God will hear me.

Psalm 5:3

3 My voice shalt thou hear in the morning, O LORD; in the morning will I direct my prayer unto thee, and will look up.

8.2 Stay in God and wait for him

Believers must be rooted and grounded in love (Ephesians 3:17). They must also expect that God will do great things for them. Many of the things God will do for them will be beyond their expectations, so they must wait on him (Ephesians 3:20).

Ephesians 3:14-21

14 For this cause I bow my knees unto the Father of our Lord Jesus Christ, 15 Of whom the whole family in heaven and earth is named, 16 That he would grant you, according to the riches of his glory, to be strengthened with might by his Spirit *in the inner man; ¹⁷ That Christ may dwell in your hearts by faith; that ye, being rooted and grounded in love, ¹⁸ May be able to comprehend with all saints what are the breadth, and length, and depth, and height; ¹⁹ And to know the love of Christ, which passeth knowledge, that ye might be filled with all the fullness of God. ²⁰ Now unto him that is able to do exceeding abundantly above all that we ask or think, according to the power that worketh in us, ²¹ Unto him be glory in the church by Christ Jesus throughout all ages, world without end. Amen.*

8.3 All things work together for God

Whenever believers wait on God, they must expect that great things will happen for them. They should expect that all things will work in their favor, as they have God on their side. As long as God is on the side of the believers, they will be victorious.

Romans 8:28

²⁸ And we know that all things work together for good to them that love God, to them who are the called according to his purpose.

9. Know his Word as you wait

Ignorance will drive people away from God, but knowledge of his Word draws them closer to him. It is God's intention that everyone know his Word, so that they will use it both in season and out of season. Believers must constantly share God's Word as often as they can, since others need to know his Word for them to become saved and for believers' faith to grow.

9.1 Share God's Word with others

When persons attend church services, they receive knowledge of God's Word. However, they are then expected to share his Word with others.

2 Timothy 4:2-4

2 Preach the word; be instant in season, out of season; reprove, rebuke, exhort with all long suffering and doctrine. 3 For the time will come when they will not endure sound doctrine; but after their own lusts shall they heap to themselves teachers, having itching ears; 4 And they shall turn away their ears from the truth, and shall be turned unto fables.

9.2 Study God's Word

Every believer must know God's Word for themselves. They must make it a personal sacrifice to go through the scriptures and gain a personal knowledge of the Word, so that when they have to apply the Word, they operate as skilled soldiers, defending God's truth.

2 Timothy 2:15

15 Study to shew thyself approved unto God, a workman that needeth not to be ashamed, rightly dividing the word of truth.

9.3 Meditate on God's Word

God reminded Joshua to meditate on his Word. As Joshua meditated on the Word of God, he obtained great success.

Joshua 1:7-8

7 Only be thou strong and very courageous, that thou mayest observe to do according to all the law, which Moses my servant commanded thee: turn not from it to the right hand or to the left, that thou mayest prosper withersoever thou goest. 8 This book of the law shall not depart out of thy mouth; but thou shalt meditate therein day and night, that thou mayest observe to do according to all that is written therein: for then thou shalt make thy way prosperous, and then thou shalt have good success.

Besides reading God's Word, persons must take time to do a thorough review of the scriptures. When they meditate on his Word, they have a better understanding of his promises for them and when he wants them to wait on him.

9.4 God will teach believers his truth as they wait on him

Believers must be willing to ask God to teach them his truth as they wait on him.

Psalm 25:5

5 Lead me in thy truth, and teach me: for thou art the God of my salvation; on thee do I wait all the day.

Psalm 130:5-6

5 I wait for the LORD, my soul doth wait, and in his word do I hope. 6 My soul waiteth for the Lord more than they that watch for the morning: I say, more than they that watch for the morning.

9.5 Faith comes alive through hearing God's Word

If anyone wants to build their faith, they must be prepared to know more of God's Word. They must position themselves to hear his Word continuously, and not as a one-off occasion.

Romans 10:14-17

14 How then shall they call on him in whom they have not believed? and how shall they believe in him of whom they have not heard? and how shall they hear without a preacher? 15 And how shall they preach, except they be sent? as it is written, How beautiful are the feet of them that preach the gospel of peace, and bring glad tidings of good things! 16 But they have not all obeyed the gospel. For Esaias saith, Lord, who hath believed our report? 17 So then faith cometh by hearing, and hearing by the word of God.

10. Waiting on God for wisdom

Many persons attend learning institutions to increase their knowledge. As persons work and get involved in daily activities, their understanding grows. As persons seek God and wait on him, they experience that their wisdom and knowledge grows. Sometimes, the growth of their wisdom and knowledge is a surprise to other persons who knew them many years ago.

10.1 Ordinary fishermen were empowered

After the believers waited in the upper room, the Lord filled them with the Holy Spirit (Acts 1:4-8; 2:1-5). These servants of God were charged with boldness and wisdom, and they did many things that caused persons to marvel at them. However, these disciples waited on the Lord for the infilling of his Spirit upon them. As they operated under the power and wisdom of the Holy Spirit, many persons were astonished. God wants to do something similar for every believer who waits upon him.

As Peter and John were doing the works that Jesus commanded them to do, many persons were saved and healed. The things that Peter and John were doing were surprising to many religious leaders, who questioned their actions. However, these religious leaders could not find any fault in them, since Peter and John were now operating under the power and wisdom of the Holy Spirit they had waited for.

Acts 4:8-21

8 Then Peter, filled with the Holy Ghost, said unto them, Ye rulers of the people, and elders of Israel, 9 If we this day be examined of the good deed done to the impotent man, by what means he is made whole; 10 Be it known unto you all, and to all the people of Israel, that by the name of Jesus Christ of Nazareth, whom ye crucified, whom God raised from the dead, even by him doth this man stand here before you whole. 11 This is the stone which was set at naught of you builders, which is become the head of the corner. 12 Neither is there salvation in any other: for there is none other name under heaven given among men, whereby we must be saved.

13 Now when they saw the boldness of Peter and John, and perceived that they were unlearned and ignorant men, they marveled; and they took knowledge of them, that they had been with Jesus. 14 And beholding the man which was healed standing with them, they could say nothing against it. 15 But when they had commanded them to go aside out of the council, they conferred among themselves, 16 Saying, What shall we do to these men? for that indeed a notable miracle hath been done by them is manifest to all them that dwell in Jerusalem; and we cannot deny it. 17 But that it spread no further among the people, let us straitly threaten them that they speak henceforth to no man in this name.

18 And they called them, and commanded them not to speak at all nor teach in the name of Jesus. 19 But Peter and John answered and said unto them, whether it be right in the sight of God to hearken unto you more than unto God, judge ye. 20 For we cannot but speak the things which we have seen and heard. 21 So when they had further threatened them, they let them go, finding nothing how they might punish them, because of the people: for all men glorified God for that which was done.

10.2 David advised Solomon that God would give him wisdom

There were many great leaders who operated in their own strength. However, David encouraged his son Solomon to seek God, and God would make him prosperous and wise as he continued to build God's temple. Indeed, to continue the work of the Lord, people need the wisdom of God.

1 Chronicles 22:11-13

11 Now, my son, the LORD be with thee; and prosper thou, and build the house of the LORD thy God, as he hath said of thee. 12 Only the LORD give thee wisdom and understanding, and give thee charge concerning Israel, that thou mayest keep the law of the LORD thy God. 13 Then shalt thou prosper, if thou takest heed to fulfil the statutes and judgments which the LORD charged Moses with concerning Israel: be strong, and of good courage; dread not, nor be dismayed.

Learning institutions are geared to equip persons to increase their knowledge. However, everyone must make it their personal responsibility to increase their knowledge, since the learning institution will not be able to provide them with information on every single thing. Common sense is something that will not be taught at learning institutions, so everyone must move away from ignorance and learn about the basic things they must know and do. Wisdom may not always come easily to persons.

Proverbs 16:16

16 How much better is it to get wisdom than gold! and to get understanding rather to be chosen than silver!

Table 1. Explanation of wisdom, knowledge, and understanding

Term	Explanation
Wisdom	Being wise, experience and knowledge together with the power of applying them critically or practically, prudence.
Knowledge	Knowing, familiarity gained by experience, intelligence, acquaintance with fact, clear perception of fact.
Understanding	Knowing, intelligent, having insight, power of apprehension.

(Extract from *The Concise Oxford Dictionary*, 5th edition, 1964)

When persons align themselves with mentors, their wisdom often improves. Many mentors will share their experiences and knowledge of how many things can be done easily and at a professional standard. A great number of younger persons and apprentices are blessed today because they have garnered much from their mentors.

"A mentor is usually someone who has particular relevant experience, knowledge, or skills, and maybe more senior than the person being mentored. The relationship is often specific to a period of transition as someone enters a new role or takes on new responsibilities that are within the mentor's own experience" (Nicholson & Baker, 2013).

10.3 Solomon asked God for wisdom

Solomon took the advice of his father, David, and as he was praying, God asked what he needed (2 Chronicles 1:7). He was quick to respond to God's request, asking God for wisdom and knowledge to lead the children of Israel (2 Chronicles 1:10). This was a son who understood what his father had taught him, and he also understood that to lead the people of God, he could not do it in his own knowledge. Therefore, God granted Solomon what he asked for, and he also gave Solomon wealth (2 Chronicles 1:11-12).

When believers are concerned about the work of the Lord, they often get more than what they asked for. God's resources are unlimited and no one individual can exhaust them.

2 Chronicles 1:1-13

¹And Solomon the son of David was strengthened in his kingdom, and the LORD his God was with him, and magnified him exceedingly. ²Then Solomon spake unto all Israel, to the captains of thousands and of hundreds, and to the judges, and to every governor in all Israel, the chief of the fathers. ³So Solomon, and all the congregation with him, went to the high place that was at Gibeon; for there was the tabernacle of the congregation of God, which Moses the servant of the LORD had made in the wilderness. ⁴But the ark of God had David brought up from Kirjathjearim to the place which David had prepared for it: for he had pitched a tent for it at Jerusalem. ⁵Moreover the brazen altar, that Bezaleel the son of Uri, the son of Hur, had made, he put before the tabernacle of the LORD: and Solomon and the congregation sought unto it.

⁶And Solomon went up thither to the brazen altar before the LORD, which was at the tabernacle of the congregation, and offered a thousand burnt offerings upon it. ⁷In that night did God appear unto Solomon, and said unto him, Ask what I shall give thee. ⁸And Solomon said unto God, Thou hast shewed great mercy unto David my father, and hast made me to reign in his stead. ⁹Now, O LORD God, let thy promise unto David my father be established: for thou hast made me king over a people like the dust of the earth in multitude. ¹⁰Give me now wisdom and knowledge that I may go out and come in before this people: for who can judge this thy people that is so great?

¹¹And God said to Solomon, Because this was in thine heart, and thou hast not asked riches, wealth, or honour, nor the life of thine enemies, neither yet hast asked long life; but hast asked wisdom and knowledge for thyself, that thou mayest judge my people, over whom I have made thee king: ¹²Wisdom and knowledge is granted unto thee; and I will give thee riches, and wealth, and honour, such as none of the kings have had that have been before thee, neither shall there any after thee have the like. ¹³Then Solomon came from his journey to the high place that was at Gibeon to Jerusalem, from before the tabernacle of the congregation, and reigned over Israel.

King Solomon's relationship with God was cemented, and he reigned over Israel (2 Chronicles 1:13). God was on the side of this wise man, and Solomon therefore became wealthy. This all happened as Solomon put God first, waited on God in the temple, and allowed God to bless him with wisdom and knowledge to lead those who would come under his leadership. The Lord wants to bless any person who will wait on him and seek his presence.

11. Wait on the Holy Spirit

Waiting for the Holy Spirit is an area of believers' lives that they are often impatient with. They want to do great things for God, but they do not always recognize that they need the empowerment of the Holy Spirit to do so, since they cannot win any spiritual battles if they walk in the flesh.

After Jesus' death and resurrection, some believers went back to their old traditions as they lost hope for the future. However, there were other believers who remembered that he had promised to send them the Comforter, so they waited for his promise to be fulfilled.

11.1 Jesus told the disciples about the Holy Spirit

When Jesus told the disciples about the Holy Spirit, it appeared that he was speaking a strange language to them. However, he knew that he was going to depart this earth and that the Holy Spirit would come and dwell in the lives of those who believe in him.

John 16:12-15

12 I have yet many things to say unto you, but ye cannot bear them now. 13 Howbeit when he, the Spirit of truth, is come, he will guide you into all truth: for he shall not speak of himself; but whatsoever he shall hear, that shall he speak: and he will shew you things to come. 14 He shall glorify me: for he shall receive of mine, and shall shew it unto you. 15 All things that the Father hath are mine: therefore said I that he shall take have mine, and shall shew it unto you.

11.2 Jesus commanded the believers to wait for the Holy Spirit

After Jesus' resurrection, he appeared to some believers. He spent forty days with them and taught them about the kingdom of God (Acts 1:3-4). He also commanded them not to leave Jerusalem but to tarry there until they received the gift of the Father (Acts 1:4). Jesus made a great commitment to those believers who listened to him after his resurrection, as he told them in a few days, the Holy Spirit would be with them (Acts 1:5).

Acts 1:3-8

³ To whom also he shewed himself alive after his passion by many infallible proofs, being seen of them forty days, and speaking of the things pertaining to the kingdom of God: ⁴ And, being assembled together with them, commanded them that they should not depart from Jerusalem, but wait for the promise of the Father, which, saith he, ye have heard of me. ⁵ For John truly baptized with water; but ye shall be baptized with the Holy Ghost not many days hence. ⁶ When they therefore were come together, they asked of him, saying, Lord, wilt thou at this time restore again the kingdom to Israel? ⁷ And he said unto them, It is not for you to know the times or the seasons, which the Father hath put in his own power. ⁸ But ye shall receive power, after that the Holy Ghost is come upon you: and ye shall be witnesses unto me both in Jerusalem, and in all Judaea, and in Samaria, and unto the uttermost part of the earth.

11.3 The Holy Spirit came upon the disciples

Whenever Jesus promises to do something, he will deliver. He always wants believers to wait on him, and he fulfills his promise towards them. The Holy Spirit came upon those believers who were waiting to receive it.

Acts 2:1-5

¹ And when the day of Pentecost was fully come, they were all with one accord in one place. ² And suddenly there came a sound from heaven as of a rushing mighty wind, and it filled all the house where they were sitting. ³ And there appeared unto them cloven tongues like as of fire, and it sat upon each of them. ⁴ And they were all filled with the Holy Ghost, and began to speak with other tongues, as the Spirit gave them utterance. ⁵ And there were dwelling at Jerusalem Jews, devout men, out of every nation under heaven.

The lives of those who received the Holy Spirit were changed. As persons wait on God, they must trust him to empower them with his Spirit so that they will be able to withstand the challenges of the adversary.

11.4 Believers have spiritual battles to fight

Every believer needs the Holy Spirit, as they have spiritual battles to fight. These battles cannot be won using either their physical strength or their academic knowledge. Henceforth, believers must have the full protective spiritual armor to withstand the attacks of the adversary.

Ephesians 6:10-18

[10] Finally, my brethren, be strong in the Lord, and in the power of his might. [11] Put on the whole armour of God, that ye may be able to stand against the wiles of the devil. [12] For we wrestle not against flesh and blood, but against principalities, against powers, against the rulers of the darkness of this world, against spiritual wickedness in high places. [13] Wherefore take unto you the whole armour of God that ye may be able to withstand in the evil day, and having done all, to stand. [14] Stand therefore, having your loins girt about with truth, and having on the breastplate of righteousness; [15] And your feet shod with the preparation of the gospel of peace; [16] Above all, taking the shield of faith, wherewith ye shall be able to quench all the fiery darts of the wicked. [17] And take the helmet of salvation, and the sword of the Spirit, which is the word of God: [18] Praying always with all prayer and supplication in the Spirit, and watching thereunto with all perseverance and supplication for all saints.

Believers who do not yet have the Holy Spirit must wait on God to fill them with his Spirit. No individual can purchase spiritual gifts, so they must allow God to give them his Spirit at whatever time he chooses.

12. Waiting on God increases believers' strength

The strength of people will fail. They may become tired and frustrated. However, God wants everyone to wait upon him for renewed strength. The strength he wants to give them will enable them to do extraordinary things.

12.1 God has everlasting strength

Every day, after most persons complete their main duties, they are tired. There are even some persons who are unable to complete their basic duties because they are tired. However, God is never tired, as he has everlasting strength (Isaiah 40:28). When believers are connected to God, they are also endowed with strength through which they can accomplish many things.

Isaiah 40:28-31

28 Hast thou not known? hast thou not heard, that the everlasting God, the LORD, the Creator of the ends of the earth, fainteth not, neither is weary? there is no searching of his understanding. 29 He giveth power to the faint; and to them that have no might he increaseth strength. 30 Even the youths shall faint and be weary, and the young men shall utterly fall: 31 But they that wait upon the LORD shall renew their strength; they shall mount up with wings as eagles; they shall run, and not be weary; and they shall walk, and not faint.

Figure 7. God renews the strength of those who wait on him

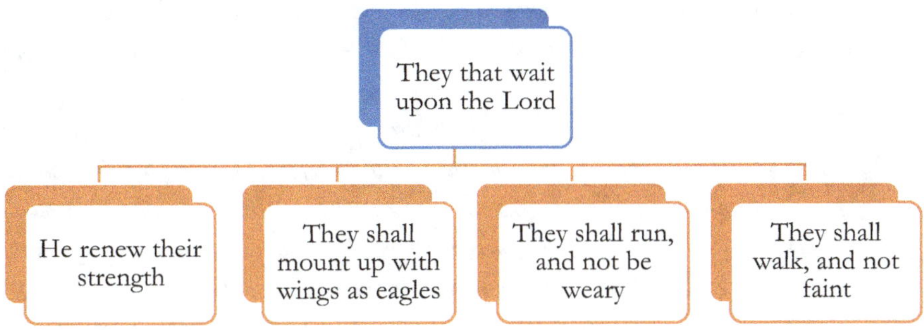

God is so loving that even when persons are weak and do not have strength, he gives strength to them (Isaiah 40:29). This should cause many persons to believe in him, as he will increase their strength whenever the need arises.

2 Corinthians 12:9-10

⁹ And he said unto me, My grace is sufficient for thee: for my strength is made perfect in weakness. Most gladly therefore will I rather glory in my infirmities, that the power of Christ may rest upon me. ¹⁰ Therefore I take pleasure in infirmities, in reproaches, in necessities, in persecutions, in distresses for Christ's sake: for when I am weak, then am I strong.

God's strength is made perfect in the believers' weakness (2 Corinthians 12:9). As believers go through their battles and wait on God, he will demonstrate his strength to protect them from danger.

12.2 Persecuted, but protected by God

The life of every believer will come under scrutiny from the adversary. Believers will be persecuted, but their God will not abandon them. While they will be struck down, God will ensure that they are not destroyed. Sometimes, when believers are going through one calamity, another calamity will come to them. However, believers must know that God will protect them and give them the strength to be victorious.

2 Corinthians 4:7-15

⁷ But we have this treasure in earthen vessels, that the excellency of the power may be of God, and not of us. ⁸ We are troubled on every side, yet not distressed; we are perplexed, but not in despair; ⁹ Persecuted, but not forsaken; cast down, but not destroyed; ¹⁰ Always bearing about in the body the dying of the Lord Jesus, that the life also of Jesus might be made manifest in our body. ¹¹ For we which live are always delivered unto death for Jesus' sake, that the life also of Jesus might be made manifest in our mortal flesh. ¹² So then death worketh in us, but life in you.

¹³ We having the same spirit of faith, according as it is written, I believed, and therefore have I spoken; we also believe, and therefore speak; ¹⁴ Knowing that he which raised up the Lord Jesus shall raise up us also by Jesus, and shall present us with you. ¹⁵ For all things are for your sakes, that the abundant grace might through the thanksgiving of many redound to the glory of God.

Every believer must stay in God, and he will be there for them. While believers are going through their battles, the Lord will give them strength to overcome their challenges and to make them successful against the attacks of the enemies (Ephesians 6:11).

Philippians 4:13

¹³ I can do all things through Christ which strengtheneth me.

13. God prospers those who wait on him

God wants to prosper those who wait on him. As believers wait on him, they must seek to know more of him and get themselves occupied in his work. The Lord will not bless idlers.

13.1 Seek God first

When believers pray to God for their provision, they must ask him to provide their daily bread (Matthew 6:11). He is always able and willing to provide for the needs of his children, but he wants them to ask him and wait for him to meet their needs.

Since God is able to provide for the fowls of the air, he is also able to provide for those who ask and wait on him. When persons seek him first, he will provide for them (Matthew 6:33).

Matthew 6:11, 25-26, 32-34

11 Give us this day our daily bread.

25 Therefore I say unto you, Take no thought for your life, what ye shall eat, or what ye shall drink; nor yet for your body, what ye shall put on. Is not the life more than meat, and the body than raiment? 26 Behold the fowls of the air: for they sow not, neither do they reap, nor gather into barns; yet your heavenly Father feedeth them. Are ye not much better than they?

32 (For after all these things do the Gentiles seek:) for your heavenly Father knoweth that ye have need of all these things. 33 But seek ye first the kingdom of God, and his righteousness; and all these things shall be added unto you. 34 Take therefore no thought for the morrow: for the morrow shall take thought for the things of itself. Sufficient unto the day is the evil thereof.

Figure 8. Waiting on God for prosperity

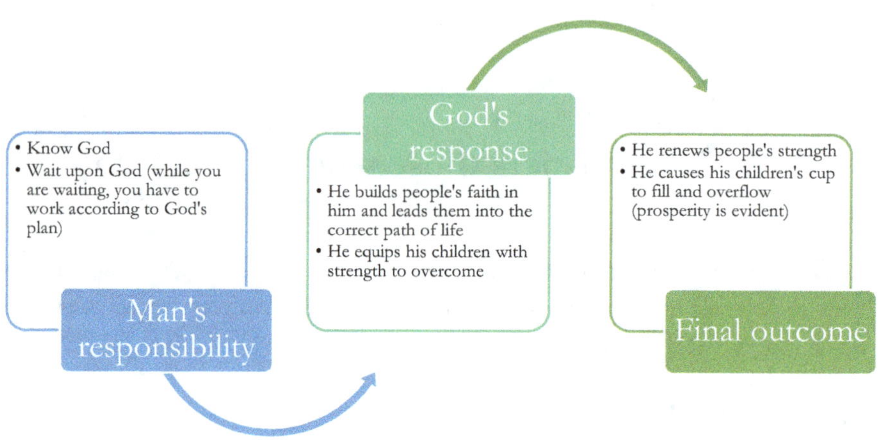

13.2 God restored Job's prosperity

Job served God and was an upright man (Job 1:1). He had many possessions, but after God gave Satan permission to try Job, he lost most of the things he once had (Job 1:8-22). This would be a frustrating position for anyone to be in. Nevertheless, Job remained faithful in God (Job 1:22). He waited on God, and his possessions were ultimately restored (Job 42:10-17). This is the very thing that God will do for those who wait on him. The waiting period may look long, but God is sure to prosper those who wait on him.

Job 42:10-17

10 And the LORD turned the captivity of Job, when he prayed for his friends: also the LORD gave Job twice as much as he had before. 11 Then came there unto him all his brethren, and all his sisters, and all they that had been of his acquaintance before, and did eat bread with him in his house: and they bemoaned him, and comforted him over all the evil that the LORD had brought upon him: every man also gave him a piece of money, and everyone an earring of gold. 12 So the LORD blessed the latter end of Job more than his beginning: for he had fourteen thousand sheep, and six thousand camels, and a thousand yoke of oxen, and a thousand she asses. 13 He had also seven sons and three daughters. 14 And he called the name of the first, Jemima; and the name of the second, Kezia; and the name of the third, Kerenhappuch. 15 And in all the land were no women found so fair as the daughters of Job: and their father gave them inheritance among their brethren. 16 After this lived Job an hundred and forty years, and saw his sons, and his sons' sons, even four generations. 17 So Job died, being old and full of days.

13.3 Fret not about wicked persons' prosperity

Sometimes, it can feel very frustrating to see how the wicked appear to be enjoying a good life while the believers struggle. However, the Word of God reminds all believers not to fret themselves concerning the prosperity of the wicked, since God will judge them accordingly (Psalm 37:5-7). As believers wait patiently on God, they will have their days of great inheritance.

Psalm 37:7-9

7 Rest in the LORD, and wait patiently for him: fret not thyself because of him who prospereth in his way, because of the man who bringeth wicked devices to pass. 8 Cease from anger, and forsake wrath: fret not thyself in any wise to do evil. 9 For evildoers shall be cut off: but those that wait upon the LORD, they shall inherit the earth.

13.4 All creation waits on God to provide for them

Beyond human beings, all other creation also depends upon God to provide for them. Many of these creations cannot move to find food for themselves, yet the Lord provides for them daily. Therefore, humans must also wait on God to meet their needs.

Psalm 104:27-28

27 These wait all upon thee; that thou mayest give them their meat in due season. 28 That thou givest them they gather: thou openest thine hand, they are filled with good.

13.5 God made Joseph prosperous

Joseph, one of Jacob's sons, went through many difficulties. He could have been frustrated, but he chose to remain in God. As he waited on the Lord, the Lord directed him into the hands of Potiphar. As Joseph worked for his master, the Lord caused the things that Joseph did to prosper. Take note that because of Joseph's relationship with the Lord, whatever he did, God caused him to prosper.

Genesis 39:2-5, 23

2 And the LORD was with Joseph, and he was a prosperous man; and he was in the house of his master the Egyptian. 3 And his master saw that the LORD was with him, and that the LORD made all that he did to prosper in his hand. 4 And Joseph found grace in his sight, and he served him: and he made him overseer over his house, and all that he had he put into his hand. 5 And it came to pass from the time that he had made him overseer in his house, and over all that he had, that the LORD blessed the Egyptian's house for Joseph's sake; and the blessing of the LORD was upon all that he had in the house, and in the field.

23 The keeper of the prison looked not to anything that was under his hand; because the LORD was with him, and that which he did, the LORD made it to prosper.

14. God knows the way and the timing

It is never God's intention to leave anyone waiting unnecessarily. Many persons think that if they have to wait a long time, it is better to cancel what they had planned to do. However, God knows the way, and he wants to carefully direct the steps of his children and prevent them from danger.

14.1 Commit your ways to God

It may be challenging, but every believer must commit their ways unto the Lord. They must allow the Lord to work through their lives and to direct their path.

Proverbs 16:1-3

[1] The preparations of the heart in man, and the answer of the tongue, is from the LORD. [2] All the ways of a man are clean in his own eyes; but the LORD weigheth the spirits. [3] Commit thy works unto the LORD, and thy thoughts shall be established.

14.2 The believers' enemies are in God's hands

When believers allow God enough time to work in their defense, the Lord will put an end to those who plan to harm them. Many persons who do wickedness believe that they will reign forever and be able to do whatever they want. However, God knows how to subdue his children's enemies.

Proverbs 16:4, 6-7

[4] The LORD hath made all things for himself: yea, even the wicked for the day of evil.
[6] By mercy and truth iniquity is purged: and by the fear of the LORD men depart from evil. [7] When a man's ways please the LORD, he maketh even his enemies to be at peace with him.

14.3 God will direct the steps of the believers

Proverbs 16:9

⁹A man's heart deviseth his way: but the LORD directeth his steps.

God wants to direct the steps of his children, but he often wishes that they will wait on him and allow him to work through their lives. When persons try to do things before God is ready for them, they often will not accomplish what the Lord has in store for them. Therefore, believers, allow God to direct your steps.

Proverbs 20:24

²⁴Man's goings are of the LORD; how can a man then understand his own way?

14.4 Trust God for directions

There are many successes and failures ahead of everyone. However, when persons trust God, he will direct their path.

Proverbs 3:5-7

⁵Trust in the LORD with all thine heart; and lean not unto thine own understanding. ⁶In all thy ways acknowledge him, and he shall direct thy paths. ⁷Be not wise in thine own eyes: fear the LORD, and depart from evil.

God wants his children to have total reliance on him as he protects and provides for them.

14.5 The Lord has a plan for everyone's life

When persons are experiencing problems, they often believe that God has forgotten them. Some persons even believe that their time here on this earth is all a waste of time. However, God has a plan for every individual. He knows what he wants everyone to do.

Jeremiah 29:11-12

¹¹For I know the thoughts that I think toward you, saith the LORD, thoughts of peace, and not of evil, to give you an expected end. ¹²Then shall ye call upon me, and ye shall go and pray unto me, and I will hearken unto you.

15. God is glorified through Lazarus' death

The scriptures provide evidence that Jesus and Lazarus were friends (John 11:3). Jesus received word that Lazarus was severely ill, but he did not do anything to immediately help his friend who was sick. Jesus' response was very strange to many persons. The Lord was not troubled about Lazarus' sickness or death, because he had something great planned (John 11:4).

John 11:1-3

1 Now a certain man was sick, named Lazarus, of Bethany, the town of Mary and her sister Martha. 2 (It was that Mary which anointed the Lord with ointment, and wiped his feet with her hair, whose brother Lazarus was sick.) 3 Therefore his sisters sent unto him, saying, Lord, behold, he whom thou lovest is sick. 4 When Jesus heard that, he said, This sickness is not unto death, but for the glory of God, that the Son of God might be glorified thereby.

15.1 Waiting on Jesus is always worthwhile

After Jesus heard of Lazarus' death, he did not take any action to help his friend. This may appear strange, but Jesus had his own plans. Jesus chose to go through a place where his life was threatened, and he did not mind doing that while Lazarus was in poor health (John 11:6-9).

Figure 9. Jesus' initial actions after hearing of Lazarus' sickness

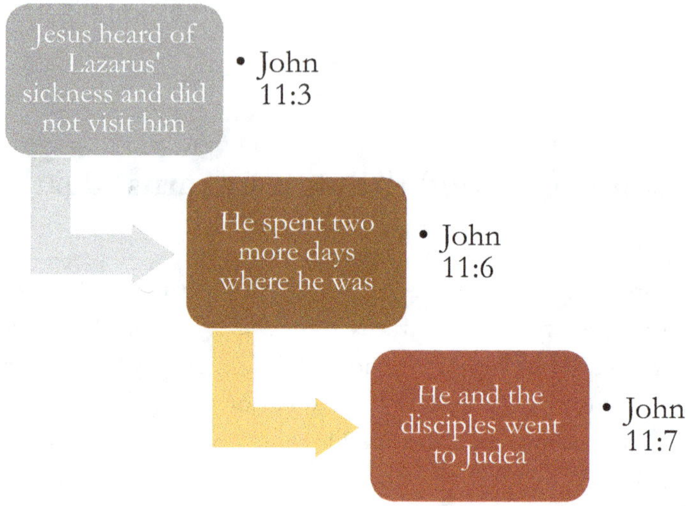

John 11:5-16

5 Now Jesus loved Martha, and her sister, and Lazarus. 6 When he had heard therefore that he was sick, he abode two days still in the same place where he was. 7 Then after that saith he to his disciples, Let us go into Judaea again. 8 His disciples say unto him, Master, the Jews of late sought to stone thee; and goest thou thither again? 9 Jesus answered, Are there not twelve hours in the day? If any man walks in the day, he stumbleth not, because he seeth the light of this world. 10 But if a man walks in the night, he stumbleth, because there is no light in him. 11 These things said he: and after that he saith unto them, our friend Lazarus sleepeth; but I go, that I may awake him out of sleep. 12 Then said his disciples, Lord, if he sleep, he shall do well. 13 Howbeit Jesus spake of his death: but they thought that he had spoken of taking of rest in sleep. 14 Then said Jesus unto them plainly, Lazarus is dead. 15 And I am glad for your sakes that I was not there, to the intent ye may believe; nevertheless let us go unto him. 16 Then said Thomas, which is called Didymus, unto his fellow disciples, Let us also go, that we may die with him.

15.2 Jesus brought an end to the waiting

After Jesus returned from Judea, he was ready to meet with Mary and Martha. He was now ready to perform a miracle so that his Father would be gloried. Jesus was about to send an important message to people that while they may think they are waiting a long time for God to meet their needs, he will show up, and one action from God will fix everything they have been waiting for.

Figure 10. When Jesus was ready to visit Lazarus, what was Lazarus' condition?

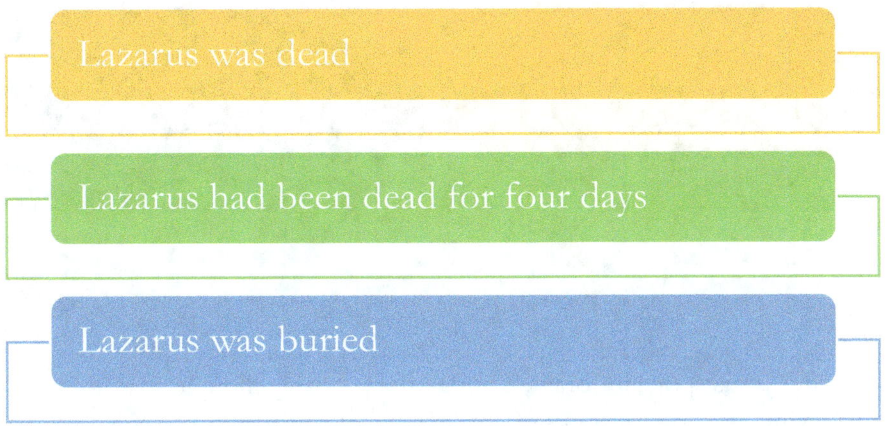

From an ordinary man's point of view, it looked like Jesus wasted his time to come and see Lazarus (John 11:17). Take note, Bethany was only about two miles from Jerusalem, and yet Jesus did not show up until four days after Lazarus died (John 11:18). The family of Lazarus had also buried him, so it seemed as if Jesus' visit to the family was no longer important.

John 11:17-19

17 Then when Jesus came, he found that he had lain in the grave four days already. 18 Now Bethany was nigh unto Jerusalem, about fifteen furlongs off: 19 and many of the Jews came to Martha and Mary, to comfort them concerning their brother.

15.3 Martha exercised faith in Jesus

Although her brother was dead and buried, Martha was still expecting great things to happen. She stated the facts to Jesus that her brother was dead, but if Jesus would ask his Father anything, then it would be done (John 11:21-22). Jesus responded to Martha's statement with great assurance that something great was about to happen for those who would wait and trust him (John 11:23).

Figure 11. Martha's expectation of Jesus and Jesus' positive assurance to her (John 11:22-23)

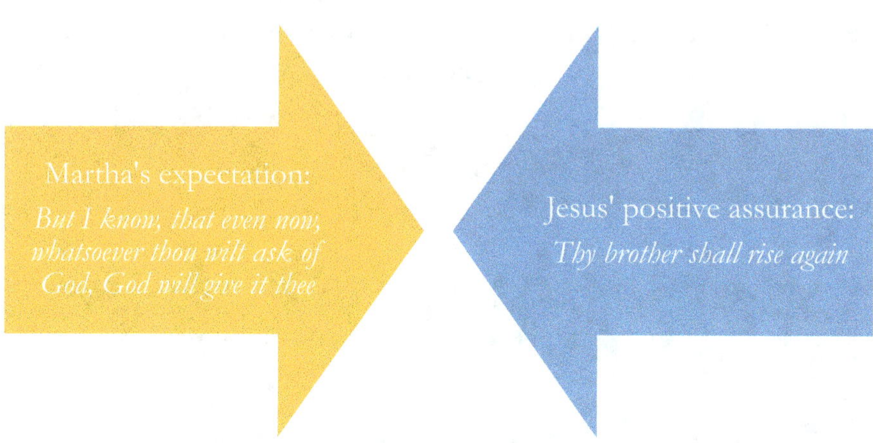

After Jesus spoke in John 11:23, Martha probably thought that Jesus was just giving her a nice response to make her feel comforted.

John 11:20-23

20 Then Martha, as soon as she heard that Jesus was coming, went and met him: but Mary sat still in the house. 21 Then said Martha unto Jesus, Lord, if thou hadst been here, my brother had not died. 22 But I know, that even now, whatsoever thou wilt ask of God, God will give it thee. 23 Jesus saith unto her, Thy brother shall rise again.

15.4 Mary and Martha's waiting was over

While Mary and Martha waited four days for Jesus to visit them, their wait was about to be over. Jesus had arrived, and great things were to happen. When persons wait on God and he shows up, he can turn any situation around. God will even make things that were dead come alive, if he wants his children to have those things. Lazarus was taken out of the grave and brought back to life because Jesus was ready for his Father to be glorified through this miracle.

John 11:24-37

24 Martha saith unto him, I know that he shall rise again in the resurrection at the last day. 25 Jesus said unto her, I am the resurrection, and the life: he that believeth in me, though he were dead, yet shall he live: 26 And whosoever liveth and believeth in me shall never die. Believest thou this? 27 She saith unto him, Yea, Lord: I believe that thou art the Christ, the Son of God, which should come into the world. 28 And when she had so said, she went her way, and called Mary her sister secretly, saying, The Master is come, and calleth for thee. 29 As soon as she heard that, she arose quickly, and came unto him.

30 Now Jesus was not yet come into the town, but was in that place where Martha met him. 31 The Jews then which were with her in the house, and comforted her, when they saw Mary, that she rose up hastily and went out, followed her, saying, She goeth unto the grave to weep there. 32 Then when Mary was come where Jesus was, and saw him, she fell down at his feet, saying unto him, Lord, if thou hadst been here, my brother had not died. 33 When Jesus therefore saw her weeping, and the Jews also weeping which came with her, he groaned in the spirit, and was troubled. 34 And said, Where have ye laid him? They said unto him, Lord, come and see. 35 Jesus wept. 36 Then said the Jews, Behold how he loved him! 37 And some of them said, Could not this man, which opened the eyes of the blind, have caused that even this man should not have died?

Lazarus' death and Jesus' response ought to serve as a great reminder to believers that if they wait on God, then God can show up and do what only he can do. If God sees the situation fit to restore something that was lost or dead, then he has the ability to restore that thing. Therefore, put your trust in God and wait on him to do miracles in your life. Waiting on God is always profitable.

Reference list

Fowler, H. W., & Fowler, F. G. (1964). *The Concise Oxford Dictionary* (5th ed.). Oxford University Press.

Nicholson, F., & Baker, C. (2013). *Certification in risk management assurance.* Institute of Internal Auditors Research Foundation (IIARF).

About the Author

It might appear that God took too long to do certain things for Geary Reid, but over the years, he has learned to wait on God. Many times, when he did things before God was ready, he became frustrated. This frustration often caused him to wonder and blame himself for making the wrong decision. However, after many years of failed attempts, Reid decided to let God be in charge of whatever situation confronts him, and he now waits for God to give him the victory.

Before Geary Reid came to know Jesus as his personal Savior, he was very impatient. He often wanted many things to happen swiftly and in his own way, but he then learned to wait on God.

After seeing what God will do for those who wait on him, Rev. Reid is no longer anxious, but places his concerns in the hands of a God who is able and capable of making great things happen. It can be difficult sometimes to wait on God, especially when there are so many things to be done, but when Reid has waited on God, he has received victories that would have been impossible if he had tried to do those things in his own strength and wisdom.

Since Reid knows that he does not know the future, he relaxes and allows God to work things out for him. However, in the meantime, while Reid waits, he will pray unto a God who hears and answers his children. He also worships the Lord for those things that he is waiting to see materialized. He does not worship God only for the things he can get from God, but because of who the Lord is to him.

Spending more time with the Word of God has allowed Geary Reid to have a greater appreciation for waiting on God. He has seen that God has done great things for persons who wait on him, so he practices waiting on God, as he knows that God knows best for his life.

Waiting on God provides renewed strength for persons, so Geary Reid is waiting because he wants to have strength to soar like the eagle. He wants to go places he has never gone before. He expects to receive things he has never received before, so he will continue to wait on God.

God has performed miracles for many persons who waited for him. So, Rev. Reid will continue to do the works of the Lord, and as he serves the Lord, he will wait for those things that only God can make happen for him.

This page is intentionally left blank.

This page is intentionally left blank.

This page is intentionally left blank.

This page is intentionally left blank.

This page is intentionally left blank.

This page is intentionally left blank.

This page is intentionally left blank.

This page is intentionally left blank.

This page is intentionally left blank.